GOD ACCORDING TO PSALM 23

Oteng Montshiti

GOD ACCORDING TO PSALM 23
COPYRIGHT ©2019
CONTACT ADDRESS: OTENG MONTSHITI
P O BOX M1139
KANYE
BOTSWANA

E-MAIL ADDRESS: otengmontshiti@gmail.com
Contact number: (+267) 74 644 954

Table of contents

Acknowledgements
Writing a book is not an easy task. Therefore I would like to thank our lord Jesus Christ, my family especially my lovely wife who supported me.

Chapter 1
Who is God?

There was a man who lived in a very far country. He was a tall, slim, short man with grey hair. His name was Mr. John. Mr. John had twin daughters namely Radan and Mary.

Radan was short and fleshy girl with dark black hair and Mary had dark black hair, she was tall with a curvy body. They were 20 years old.

One day as they were having diner, their

father glanced at them and throw a question at them, he asked with a wide grin,

"My child, if you are asked to say who I am, what would you say,"

"I would say, you are the

greatest Daddy and our protector," Mary answered.

"What about you Radan?" he stared at her.

"I would say, you are the provider and counsellor," Radan replied.

Mr John paused for few minutes drumming his fingers on the table and said,

"You are correct, my children," as he lifted a steaming cup of black coffee to his mouth.

When it comes to the

issue of faith we all know God differently because he interact with us differently. He do that because we are not at the same level of faith. Therefore, we view him differently. Some know him as the great provider.

Other know him as the all wise and all-knowing God. Moses knew him as the great who I am. The question is who is God to you? David knew him as his shepherd.

Now let's explain who

and what God is
according to
King David in
Psalm 23 under
the powerful
influence of the
Holy Spirit;

Chapter 2

Ps 23:1, The LORD *is* my shepherd; I shall not want. (KJV)

As the sunlight flooded our round mud house at the cattle post through a crack in the wall I threw my blankets away, rubbed my sleepy eyes and gradually rolled out of my bed. Dress up and strolled across the mud floor and threw the door open. I washed my face using some water in cup and went to the kraal. I was a shepherd by then looking after my family livestock or sheep to be precise.

Every day when I entered the kraal they would glanced up at me and break down in tears and cry.

Not tears of sorrow but tears of joy. Some would leap up in the midair and licked my hands. Some would brushed the skin against my garments. Others would stand in front of me stared at me with trust.

And I would brush them as I feed them. They knew in their hearts that I was their shepherd. And I would defend their lives with mine. When an enemy comes I would get out of comfort zone and stood on the gap.

I would say, "If you want to kill them kill me first."

In a similar manner as a child of God, God is your shepherd. He is looking over your lives twenty four hours, non-stop.

When you are fast asleep and the enemy tries to strike you he will defend you with everything he has. That is what we call Godly intervention.

There is a certain sister who shared her

dream with us. She said she had a dream whereby somebody wanted to feed her with food. As we all know that eating in the dreams is very wrong she woke up before she could eat those food and sat straight in her bed with her heart racing in her chest. It was Godly intervention and it is part of shepherding assignment of God.

When you are with God you must trust

him hundred percent that is to say, trusting him in good and in bad times alike.

When you fellowship with God you must trust his abilities. He is not a man he cannot lie. That is why when I interacted with those sheep, they did not sense danger at all cost but sensed love. They knew that when I am with them they are safe and sound.

But God is inviting you to allow him to be your shepherd.

To accept him as your Lord and savior.

Then you can take it from there. He is not gate crasher he goes where is he is love and welcomed or permitted. In simple words, you must agree to work with him in your life. He needs your permission. You can't walk with somebody harmoniously if you don't love or welcome him or her in your life that is why prayer of salvation is very important.

When you are born again you become one of his sheep. From there the process of trust can be put into place because you can't trust somebody you don't know. You can't trust a stranger because you don't know his or her character or the way he or she views issues pertaining life.

Before somebody can trust you, you must sacrifice something precious before him or her. That is one of the

reasons why
God gave up
Jesus Christ as
the last sacrifice
so that through
him we can be
saved. Jesus
Christ was, is
precious to God
and he will
always be.
Therefore it was
not easy for

him to give up his precious son to die for the remission of our sins. But he had no option but to release him for us. When he was brutally killed as it is written or according to the will of God, God was hurt. But he watched as his precious possession is killed but he knew in his heart if he intervene the whole world would be lost. Also he knew that the rightful thing must be done in this world and for Jesus Christ to be killed was the right thing to do before him.

My dear reader, you must trust God with your life. That is to say with everything (soul, body and spirit). You must honour with your life. He is a good shepherd who never allow any of sheep to depart from his sight.

When you allow yourself to be under the authority of God, protection, blessings, and deliverance are made available to you.

But the best thing about God is that he has given us the power of choice.

You can choose to follow him or to follow your personal desire. In other words you can choose to allow him to shepherd you or you can say, "No, God I want to shepherd myself."

In other words, you can choose to direct yourself or rely on your own strength.

God is ready to shepherd you but the burning issue is are you ready to be led? Are you ready to be in his kraal?

God will never operate against your will or desire,

John 10:27, My sheep hear my voice, and I know them, and they follow me:

Do you know why David won most his battle?

He allowed God to be his shepherd. He allowed him to guide, correct and to submit to his lordship. When you give your life to Jesus Christ you are simply saying, "God take away my strength and give me your strength or today I lean on you." It is as simple as that.

When you give your life to Jesus Christ you are saying, "God I don't trust myself I trust you. I don't trust my vision I trust your vision.

I don't walk as I will but according to your will. I don't speak as I will but as you will or desire. I don't interact with people the way I wish but according to your wish." In other words you put your plans aside and let his plans prevail in your life. Because a sheep has no plan of its own, it relies entirely on the plans of the shepherd.

When God is your shepherd you will look at him with total trust and submission.

But today it is a different story people look at God with distrust and doubt. And that is the most destructive element in the life of a believer.

When you are with God you can't lack

because he is a blessing. If you accept Jesus Christ as your lord and your savior you are automatically blessed. When we were at school we were taught about magnetic and non-magnetic materials.

Magnetic materials attract materials made of iron and non-magnetic materials lack that capability. God is like a magnet when you serve him in truth and in spirit or with love, I am telling you struggle is over.

What you will meet in your spiritual walk will be there to strengthen you not to destroy you.

For example, when Jesus Christ was walking upon the surface of the earth people just

came to him
without struggle.
Do you know
why? He was
carrying Holy
Spirit in his heart
and Holy Spirit
is God.

One day, a
certain man
glanced down at
his tittle girl of
ten years

and asked her, "my lovely daughter what makes you to love me?"

His daughter glanced up at his Dad and said, "I am content when I am with you. You give me love, peace and joy.

That is the best about you," she replied squeezing his hand. And his father's heart drummed in his chest with joy and happiness.

You see God is the greatest Daddy ever.

When you are with him you must be content or fulfilled. His love is enough to fill your heart with contentment. You must be content the way you are in him. If somebody is bitter, envy, confused and is full of self-doubt etc. he or she lacks Godly love. And Godly love give birth to contentment in life.

Do you know why rich people in this world want to become richer and richer? They lack Godly love in the hearts. They worship money, fame, wealth etc. instead of God. That is to say, the position that was supposed to be occupied by God in their hearts is occupied by the love of

money, wealth
and fame,
instead of being
headquarters of
Godly love.
People of God,
God is greater
than wealth,
fame and money.

If you are not
content in life
you will want
more and more.

And the more you get is the more you are destroyed. You will never enjoy peace in your life. Therefore, it is very important to love God so that you can be content and lack nothing in your life.

<u>Chapter 3</u>

Ps 23:2, He maketh me to lie down in green pastures: he leadeth me beside the still waters. (KJV)

After feeding my sheep I would lead them outside to green pastures and clean water to quench their thirst. As I am leading them like that they would just listen to my instructions and obey them. Because a sheep cannot make judgement on its own it depend on the judgement of the shepherd.

I am a human being with limitations but God has no limitation. Therefore, the best person who knows your life is the Lord. He knows your beginnings and endings. To make matters interesting he knows where your blessing are. So the best you can do for yourself is to surrender your life to God and let him to take you to unbelievable dimension of success and prosperity.

He will never mislead you therefore, the best thing is to submit yourself to the Lord. And allow him to reshape your life and destiny and lead you there. You must totally enter into rest. To enter into rest means to be at peace and the like. That is to stop your works and allow the work of God to begin in your life. You must not be headquarters of jealousy, bitterness, and the like in order to receive from him.

God knows where your breakthrough, healing and the like are and he knows how to pass them to you. Therefore, you must be at rest. To be at rest is when you are at peace in your heart even if the environment suggest the opposite because you know that God is in control.

<u>Chapter 4</u>

Ps 23:3, He restoreth my soul: (KJV)

When you are born again what become born again is your spirit. It is restored to the original position of God.

Remember, man was created in the likeness of God. And the likeness of God is the nature of God. His nature is righteousness, holiness, faithfulness etc. but when you are not born again it is impossible to fulfil your mandate or divine assignment because you need the leadership of the Holy Spirit to do that.

You need the aid of the Holy Spirit to take

away your former man or human nature and put on the nature of God. Human nature is very destructive because it include the following; the lust of the flesh, lying, revenge and the like.

Remember God head consist of Jesus Christ, the Father and the Holy Spirit. And this is a demonstration that the completeness of God is made up of the above mentioned persons.

Without Jesus Christ or the Holy Spirit God is in complete. Similarly, a human being is made up of three department namely body, soul and spirit.

At new birth as I have said earlier what is

born again is your spirit but your soul (mind, will power and emotions) is not born again. Then, the most important thing must take place, your soul must be transformed through the word of God.

The only tool that God has given to us as his children to restore our soul is the power of the word of God. As you eat the word of God and meditate upon it you will be transformed in your mind to think and act like God.

When you think like God you will automatically see like him, love like him and walk like him.

If your spirit want to do the will of God but your soul is acting in the opposite direction you can't fulfil the mandate or assignment of God here on earth. Soul has no power of its own but it relies entirely on both the body and spirit. It is the middle man or the link between your body and spirit.

If your spirit is not full of the word the body will influence your soul to do carnally things or human desires.

According to the will of God your spirit must influence your soul but when you are

not born again
your body
influences you.
But when you
are born again
your spirit carry
your soul along
as the spirit leads
you to fulfil the
will of God.

<u>Chapter 5</u>

Ps 23:3, he leadeth me in the paths of righteousness for his name's sake. (KJV)

There are many spiritual gifts and righteousness is one of them.

Righteousness is given freely by God to his children at new birth.Therefore, you must never boast about it. When it comes to issue of faith Jesus Christ fought for our salvation at the cross of Calvary. And there is no human effort in the equation. Righteousness does not come because of your personal effort or strength but you are aided by the spirit of God. In simple words, it is the condition of being upright before God.

If you reject drunkards, prostitutes and many other people because you are upright before God it is not divine righteousness. It is self-righteousness and anyone who is full of self-righteousness

never pleases
the Lord.

When you
receive a gift
from God it is
not for your
personal benefit
but it is for
betterment of
mankind. In
simple words,
you are given
blessings to go

and help others to discover your source (God). In this way you must help others to discover Jesus Christ and receive him and ultimately they will receive salvation and live righteous life before God.

<u>Chapter 6</u>

Ps 23:4, Yea, though I walk through the valley of the shadow of death, I will fear no evil: for thou *art* with me; (KJV)

This is very interesting

because God did not promised us a smooth road but a bumpy road. Life is a mixture of good and bad times. What differentiate great people is how they view challenges or situations.

They know that challenges are there to strengthen them and they know that God is greater than those challenges.

Whatever you are going through a challenge be of good cheer Jesus Christ has overcome the world for you. The world means system of doing things. Jesus Christ overcame all challenges for us and what is left for us is to view situations as mere shadows. Shadows are not real things.

The real things
are things Jesus
Christ overcame
for us on the
cross.

When you are
facing poverty
just say, "Come
on poverty, Jesus
Christ is bigger
than you." If it is
sickness just say,

"Sickness come on Jesus Christ overcame you for me on the cross." If it is death just say, "Come on death, I am not afraid of you Jesus Christ overcame you on the cross."

Do you know the real death? It is when you are not born again because you can't fulfil your spiritual mandate here on earth. Real death is when you die and you are separated from God for eternity.

If you are a child of God and you die you know it is upliftment because you are going to rest for eternity at the feet of Jesus Christ. You will still be connected to God in the dimension of eternity.

If you are a child
of God you have
already
overcame death.
You are a
spiritual person
here on earth.
Fear not the
Lord is with
you.

Chapter 7

Psalm 23:4 thy rod and thy staff they comfort me. (KJV)

The rod refers to the word of God and the word of God is Jesus Christ who is sitting at the right hand of the father.

Isa 11:1, And there shall come forth a rod out of the stem of Jesse, and a Branch shall grow out of his roots:

Life without the word of god is empty

and meaningless. The word of God is a tool of comfort. That is to say, if you are wounded be of good cheer you have the word of God to comfort you.

When I was still outside the kingdom of

God I used to feel sick regularly I was stressed and there was no permanent solution. But immediately when I encountered Jesus Christ my life changed forever.

Whenever I am pained in my heart I break down in prayer and cry unto the Lord. Then, I would grab the word of God and feed on it and the word will give me peace and comfort beyond human imagination.

Even if there are too much disturbance around me but I will manage to maintain peace and comfort in my heart. To sail through the storms of life you need inner peace and it is only found in Jesus Christ your shepherd.

<u>Chapter 8</u>

Ps 23:5, Thou preparest a table before me in the presence of mine enemies:(KJV)

In this world there will always be people hunting your life or wanting to destroy your life. Whether you like it or not. That is how life was programmed. Jesus Christ had people who wanted to destroy his life left, right and center. When they thought they had finished him once and for all when he was crucified on the cross God did not kill his enemies. No! Instead he allowed them to live and see the glory of God. After three days Jesus Christ resurrected from the dead.

He overcome the power of death or the grave.

When Joseph was thrown in the dry pit and in the dark rooms of prison God did not kill those who imprisoned him.

Instead he kept them until he ascended to the throne. And when they needed his help he did not use his position to revenge but he used it as a pulpit to preach forgiveness and love.

When you are a child of God don't expect God to kill your enemies he will keep them to see you as you excel in life or move from glory to glory. The most important thing is to hold onto your salvation or build your

relationship
with him.

When Job was
going through
affliction and
people were
mocking him,
God did not kill
them. He
allowed them to
mock him as
they wished but
when the time

was right God restored him in their presence. To make matters interesting Job even prayed for them at the end. You see how God works.

Just rejoice in the Lord when you are going through difficult times. Break in the spirit of prayer and say, "Lord, I thank you. You are on the throne. I thank you for the lives of people who are laughing at me because you are about to bless me in their presence.

Chapter 9

Psalm 23: 5, thou anointest my head with oil; my cup runneth over. (KJV)

In the bible anointing oil was a tool that was used to anoint items like chairs, table pulpits and the like. Because when something is anointed it is regarded as something that is holy. As something that has been prepared to be used by God.

Anointing is the power of God that enable us as his children to fulfill our mandate here on earth. It is very impossible to fulfil the mandate of God without anointing. The work or assignment of

God is not completed because you are well learned. It is completed because of the presence of the spirit. Many people have failed to complete their mission on earth because they have rejected the anointing of God. For example, Jesus Christ completed his earthly mission because he was anointed to do so. The name Jesus Christ means the anointed one. King David was anointed with oil before he became the king of Israel and was able to fulfil his duties or assignments. He fought so many battles in his life time and won most of them because of the anointing. Moses was able to depart the red sea because of the anointing.

When you are anointed with oil every yoke of limitation, set back, poverty, shame and like is broken, Isaiah 10:27, And it shall come to pass in that day, that his burden shall be taken away from off thy shoulder, and his yoke from off thy neck, and the yoke shall be destroyed because of the anointing.

You move from glory to glory, from

blessing to blessing and from success to success. It opens doors where it is impossible to do so. When you are anointed you attracts favours from God or attracts good things. You operate in the supernatural dimension.

You operate beyond your fellows. When you are anointed nobody can curse, bless, kill or destroy you.

However, just like oil can be polluted by soil, dusty materials anointing can be polluted.

It can be polluted by entertaining the life of sin. That is to say, fornication, adultery, unfaithfulness, unforgiveness, bitterness etc. are some of the elements that can pollute anointing in your life.

Therefore, you must live an upright life before God. Upright life means living the kind of life that embraces the nature and characters of God.

<u>Chapter 10</u>

Ps 23:6, Surely goodness and mercy shall follow me all the days of my life: (KJV)

When you love God you are automatically blessed.

Good things will just come across your path without struggle. The first thing is to seek the kingdom of God and its righteousness and all other things will be added unto you.

All wonderful and good things will just locate you and manifest in your life. People will just come to you because they see the glory of God upon your life. People will just bless you with money, cars

and other
valuable
materials
because of the
presence of God
in your heart or
life.

A certain
brother went to
sleep with a
sharp pain in his
heart because he
was owing a

certain bank and his items were about to be auctioned. As the sun flooded his room, the alarm of the clock on the headboard broke the quietness of that morning. He rolled out of his bed and engaged in the spirit of prayer. Few minutes elapsed and his phone rang, it was his friend who had read that he was in deep trouble. He helped him to get out of his predicament.

You see how a child of God operates. You just need to love God and serve him the rest he will take care of it. God knows what you are going through and his goodness is enough to set you free.

He never fails. If you are followed by the love of God no one can curse you. Nobody can kill you before your time. And above all nobody can destroy you.

Chapter 11

Psalm 23:6, and
I will dwell in
the house of the
LORD forever.
(KJV)

When the sun
slide behind the
western skies the
sheep would run
before me to

the kraal. They had many things in their minds namely comfort, warmth, food supplement and the like. They would run as fast as their little legs could carry them. During the night they would sleep in a group or came closer together to generate warm. That shows that, as children of God we must meet time and again to comfort, correct and encourage one another.

Everybody love to stay in the presence of his

father. Do you know why? Because there is safety there. There is healing there. There are blessings there. There is comfort there.

To dwell in the presence of God simply means creating

sufficient time for God. That is to say, read the word of God, praying and meditating. In other words, it is to spend your time learning his ways.

When you wake up in the morning you

should not leap out of your bed. As a child of God you must develop the habit of having fellowship with the God. When you fellowship with the Holy Spirit you get instructions from him and he will give you the ability to fulfill those instructions. The more you fellowship with the Holy Spirit the more revelations you receive from God. If you don't receive revelations from God check your

time
management or
how you manage
your time.

I am telling you
if you have a
strong
relationship with
the Lord you
will never depart
from his sight. It
will not be easy
to back slide.

Above all never stop meeting with other brethren to sharpen or feed your spirit. This can be done in the house of God or by establishing cell groups or study groups.

The end

CPSIA information can be obtained at www.ICGtesting.com
Printed in the USA
BVIW121207250719
554362EV00016B/79